WHEN LIFE GIVES YOU LEMONS, MAKE A LEGACY

PATRICIA MORGAN

LAKEVIEW
PUBLICATIONS

Copyright © 2024 by Patricia Morgan

All rights reserved.

No part of this book may be reproduced in any form or by any electronic or mechanical means, including information storage and retrieval systems, without written permission from the author, except for the use of brief quotations in a book review.

THE HOLY BIBLE, NEW INTERNATIONAL VERSION®, NIV® Copyright © 1973, 1978, 1984, 2011 by Biblica, Inc.® Used by permission. All rights reserved worldwide.

Scripture quotations from The Authorized (King James) Version. Rights in the Authorized Version in the United Kingdom are vested in the Crown. Reproduced by permission of the Crown's patentee, Cambridge University Press.

The ESV® Bible (The Holy Bible, English Standard Version®). ESV® Text Edition: 2016. Copyright © 2001 by Crossway, a publishing ministry of Good News Publishers. The ESV® text has been reproduced in cooperation with and by permission of Good News Publishers. Unauthorized reproduction of this publication is prohibited. All rights reserved.

Scripture taken from the New King James Version®. Copyright © 1982 by Thomas Nelson. Used by permission. All rights reserved.

Scripture quotations marked (CEV) are from the Contemporary English Version Copyright © 1991, 1992, 1995 by American Bible Society, Used by Permission.

Publisher: LakeView Publications
Cover Design: Bobby Barnhill
Editing: LakeView Publications
Interior Book Formatting: Craig Price & Amanda Price

CONTENTS

Introduction ix

1. When Life Gives You Lemons: Make a Stand for Others 1
2. A Mother's Cry 5
   A Mother's Cry 9
3. Invisible Scars Of The Heart 10
4. There Is Growth Through Your Pain 14
5. Knocked Down But Not Knocked Out! 18
6. Ziklag 21
7. Out Of Sync 24
8. I Dont Look Like What I Have Been Through 28
9. Help is on the way 34
10. Rizpah 38
11. Mary's Lemons: A Mother's Agony at the Crucifixion of Jesus 42
12. Hannah 46
13. From Lemons to Life: A Devotional on Faith and Restoration 49
14. Lemonade 53

Afterword 61
About the Author 65
MMAD 67
About the Publisher 69

For those who've tasted life's sour lemons, yet transformed them into something extraordinary:

This book is dedicated to you.

May your legacy be a recipe: one part hardship, twist it with determination, Add a dash of hope, zest it with creativity, Stir in compassion, and let it simmer over time.

Serve it generously to others.

May your sweet and zesty legacy linger on, inspiring generations.

WHEN LIFE GIVES YOU LEMONS, MAKE A LEGACY

INTRODUCTION

We don't always understand why certain things happen to us.

There is a proverb that says, when life gives you lemons, make lemonade. There are times of discouragement and adversity in our lives when things go wrong, even when we try to do right. Times when everything seems to be falling apart at the seams when it looks like we have come to the end of the road and have gone as far as we can. The journey may seem rough and uphill. Sometimes, life offers us lemons, leaving a bitter and sour taste in our mouths. Life is full of uncertainties and surprises, and sometimes those surprises have a negative impact (lemons) on our lives. It leaves a sour taste in our mouths.

INTRODUCTION

Bad things are sometimes out of our control; we cannot control everything that happens to us. If that were possible, we would have sweet lemonade every day. We cannot brush off or sweep adversity or misfortune under the rug. One must have an optimistic attitude, face it head-on, and turn something sour (lemons) into something sweet (lemonade). And when life offers you lemons, make lemonade.

This book shows how adversity, the struggles, and the hardships that come with it strengthened me and caused growth in my life. God is not as concerned about my comfort as He is about my purpose. His goal is not to make our lives miserable; He's pushing us into our purpose. Otherwise, you would not have moved forward without a push. He knows that you would have become comfortable where you were. The struggles that I have gone through, the hurt and pain that I have experienced, pushed me, grew me, and strengthened me.

Things inside of me could not have been birthed if God had not pushed me out of my comfort zone and into my purpose. In hindsight, I now know that God did not cause the trouble that arose in my life, but He allowed the struggle to push me into my destiny.

If someone would have told me a few years ago that I would do what I am doing today, I would not have believed them. I would have told them they were

INTRODUCTION

mistaken, but here I am doing what I was pushed to do, fulfilling my purpose, and I know that this is only the beginning. I am being stretched, growing, maturing, and getting stronger. It might not seem like you are growing and getting stronger, but you are. Allow God to push you into your destiny so that you may become all that you were created to be. I promise you will not be destroyed in the process.

> *For I know the thoughts that I think toward you, saith the Lord, thoughts of peace, and not of evil, to give you an expected end.*
>
> — JEREMIAH 29:11 KJV

> *For I know the plans I have for you, says the Lord. They are plans for good and not for disaster, to give you a future and a hope.*
>
> — JEREMIAH 29:11 NLT

> *And we know that in all things, God works for the good of those who love Him, who have been called according to his purpose.*
>
> — ROMANS 8:28 NIV

1

WHEN LIFE GIVES YOU LEMONS: MAKE A STAND FOR OTHERS

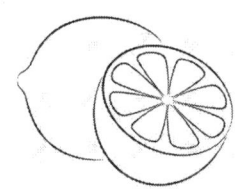

Ah, lemons. Those bright yellow fruits with a pucker-inducing punch. Sometimes, life throws them our way, unexpected and unwelcome. A setback, a loss, a disappointment – they leave us feeling sour and defeated. But what if, in those moments of bitterness, we saw an opportunity for growth, a chance to create something beautiful? My friend, here's the secret: within those lemons lies the potential for something incredibly sweet.

The proverb "When life gives you lemons, make lemonade" isn't just about turning misfortune into something positive. It's about allowing God to use those lemons to equip us for a purpose far greater.

Think about it. Lemonade, that refreshing summer drink, is born from tart lemons. It takes a little work, a little squeezing, a touch of sugar, and voila! Suddenly, the sour becomes something delightful, something that quenches thirst and brings a smile.

This is how God works in our lives. He takes our lemons, our hardships, and uses them to transform us. He may gently squeeze us through difficulties, but it's for a purpose. He wants to refine our character, strengthen our faith, and equip us to serve others.

Here's the beautiful part: He doesn't intend for us to keep this sweetness to ourselves. He wants us to use it to build a "Lemonade Stand for Life." This stand isn't about selling a drink, but about offering refreshment, encouragement, and a taste of God's love to a thirsty world.

Maybe your "lemonade" is a kind word to a discouraged neighbor. Perhaps it's using your experience to mentor someone facing a similar challenge. It could be anything – a listening ear, a helping hand, a creative act of kindness.

Imagine yourself facing a life-lemon. Perhaps it's a job loss, a broken relationship, or a health challenge. It stings, doesn't it? But what if, amidst the sourness, you heard a gentle nudge from the Holy Spirit? "There's something more here, child," He whispers. "Let me show you how to use this experience to bless others."

Suddenly, the picture changes. You see yourself not drowning in a vat of lemons, but gathering them up, one by one. God, the master chef, guides your hand as you add sugar, water, and a dash of creativity. He shows you how to transform your lemons – your struggles, disappointments, and even scars – into something refreshing and soul-satisfying.

This lemonade stand isn't just about quenching your thirst; it's about serving others. Perhaps your lemons of hardship have equipped you to offer a listening ear to a friend facing a similar challenge. Maybe you can share the lessons learned from your struggles to inspire someone else. The possibilities are endless, just like God's love and grace.

As we allow God to mold and direct us, He equips us with the perfect ingredients for our unique lemonade recipe. He shows us who needs a refreshing sip, and He fills us with the love to share it.

So, the next time life hands you a lemon, don't despair. Embrace it as an opportunity for growth. Pray for God's wisdom and allow Him to mold your experiences into something that will enrich and renew not just your own life, but the lives of those around you. Remember, the sweetest lemonade often comes from the tartest lemons.

> *For you, Lord, are good and forgiving,*
> *abounding in love to all who call on you.*
>
> — PSALM 86:5 NIV

> *We know that for those who love God all things work together for good, for those who are called according to his purpose.*
>
> — ROMANS 8:28

God is with you, even in the midst of your lemons. Trust Him, and let Him guide you to build your stand. As you read the stories of those who have taken the sourest lemons, I want to encourage you to see not just the lemons, but the stands of refreshments that God allowed them to make for others. I encourage you to join me in asking God to help you see Him always.

Dear Heavenly Father, Thank you for your unwavering love and guidance. Help us see the opportunities for growth hidden within our challenges. Equip us with the strength and wisdom to transform life's lemons into blessings for ourselves and others.

In Jesus' name, Amen.

2

A MOTHER'S CRY

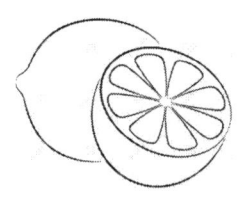

THE DATE WAS SATURDAY, October 22, 2022; it is a day that I will never forget. My sister called and told me that our mother was being transported by ambulance to the hospital. I immediately got into my car and was on my way there. While driving to the hospital, I called my pastor and informed him of the situation; he said he would be there as soon as possible.

Upon arriving at the hospital, I saw all my family members sitting in the waiting area waiting for an update on my mother's condition. I noticed another family across the corridor waiting in the next waiting area. As both families sat in total silence, waiting for updates from the doctor, suddenly, out of the silence, I heard a very distinctive, heart-wrenching cry. Upon hearing this cry, I placed my hands on my chest and said oh, Lord God, please not another one. My sister stood beside me and asked what I was talking about. I turned and looked at her and said I recognized that cry. That cry is the cry of a mother who has lost a child.

The distinctive sound of that cry - an unnatural, heartbreaking wail that tore through the sterile silence of the waiting area. It wasn't a cry of pain, but a howl of despair, a sound that spoke of a bond ripped apart, a love extinguished. Later, after what felt like an eternity but was probably closer to twenty minutes, my suspicions were confirmed. The source of that agonizing cry was a mother who had just lost her son to the cruel hand of gun violence.

Unfortunately, I am familiar with the agonizing sound of that particular cry. A mother's cry for her child is indescribable; no words can correctly identify it. If I were to describe it, it is profoundly piercing to your soul. It is a cry that depletes the oxygen from the air and has you gasping for breath. It is a cry that numbs your entire physical being.

In 2020, the United States witnessed a surge in gun violence, leaving countless families shattered. Statistics tell a grim story: over 45,000 lives were lost to gun deaths, the highest number ever recorded. Fathers undoubtedly grieve with a profound intensity, but there's a primal quality to a mother's grief after losing a child. It's a raw, visceral ache, perhaps only another mother can fully understand. When you hear that roar - a sound born from a bond ripped apart, a love extinguished by gun violence - it temporarily paralyzes you. It's a primal instinct, a forced pause in the face of unimaginable loss.

There is an invisible bond, an unspoken language, between mothers. That allows them to communicate with one another without speaking a word. We can look into one another's eyes and see the void others cannot see. We hear and know the silent cry. We feel one another pain. We walk the same pathway; some of us are further ahead on the path than others.

We are walking in a landmine of explosive emotions, trying our best not to cause collateral damage to those we may encounter. It does not matter where or what we are doing when we hear the mothers roar. We recognize it and will come to her aid.

The news hit me hard - a mother's unimaginable loss. I found her in the waiting area, a storm brewing in the silence. Without hesitation, I sat beside her. Tears welled in my own eyes as I reached for her hand. In that shared moment of grief, she leaned into me, a silent plea for comfort. I held her close, the word "momma" tumbling out in a rush. It wasn't my mother, but in her raw pain, I saw a universal ache. We sat there, a stranger and I, united by the roar of grief. I held her, and in the quiet space between us, I offered a silent prayer, hoping it would somehow reach her broken heart.

A mother's cry for her child you cannot deny, it's a piercing cry from the depths of her soul, longing for the child she no longer can hold, her cry brings tears from her eyes, as she ask the question why did her child have to die.

A mother's cry may last a while, making it impossible for her to smile, no one really comprehends her pain, life as she once knew it has forever changed.

A mother's cry is stabbing to the soul, she is broken in places where she was once whole, tears stream down her cheeks as if it was rain, yet she holds her head up high, and is not a shame.

A mother's cry is one of love, missing the gift given her from above, how long will her tears continue to flow, no one will ever know,

A mother's cry is like no another, it's different from the cry for a brother, it has a distinctive sound, it will send chills down your spine when you hear the voice of a mother crying.

3

INVISIBLE SCARS OF THE HEART

He healeth the broken in heart and bindeth up their wounds.

— PSALMS 147:3

SCARS ARE A PART OF LIFE. They come in all different shapes and sizes, each with a different story. Webster's dictionary defines a scar as a mark left by a healed wound. Some scars are visible, while others are hidden. Some are physical and emotional; the most painful scar is the one people don't see. The invisible scar on the heart that we carry deep within us leaves a spot on our soul, and they are not easy to know unless we choose to share them.

An invisible scar on the heart is like having a broken rib; it is invisible to others unless we share it. It is there and painful to our hearts. From the outside, you look fine, but there is a hidden scar that no one sees. But Jesus sees it, and he cares about our pain. He heals the hurt and the wounds in the deepest part of ourselves. Those wounds that no one else knows that we are carrying have left us with a scar.

In life, we all encounter difficulties and distress that can leave their mark on us somehow. Marks (scars) can be physical, emotional, or mental. In whatever form they show up, they are a memorandum of the battles we have fought and the journey we have traveled and crossed over.

Your scars are your beauty mark, a testament to the battles that you have fought and the challenges that you have overcome. Every scar tells a story. Your scar tells a survival story.

It was December 20, 2017, my son was murdered on his birthday, and that left a scar on my heart. The fact that I am still here to talk about it is an integral part of who I am. From the outside, I look ok, but a pain is there that no one can see. The invisible scar that I carry shows that I am a survivor. It represents strength and courage. I am proud of my mark because it shows courage and that I have endured; it is my beauty mark. It shows that I went through an ordeal and that I survived.

My scar, the invisible scar on my heart, tells a story of how I was tried and tested in the school of life. You can only tell the strength of something once it has been tested. You will only know if you can withstand the storms once you go through one. Until you are truly tested in the storms of life and experience the cuts, bruises, bumps, and scars, you won't know how strong you are. It reminds me of how God equips me to endure and rise above trouble. My scars remind me that I can take much more than I think. Not only did I experience a difficult situation, but I made it. I survived. I was able to move on rather than quit. I chose to continue living. It would help if you decided to continue living also. You can make it and rise above, too. Let me tell you that you are a lot stronger than you think.

Don't ever be afraid to show your scars, to share the story behind them. You don't have to share them with everyone. Your scars are your beauty mark, an encouragement to others. You didn't go through what you went through just for yourself. When you share your invisible scars of the heart, you also permit others to share theirs. You went through it for someone else. You can tell them how you did it when you made it to the other side. They will see your cuts, bruises, scratches, and scars and know life's misfortunes did not destroy you. And know that the weapons designed to stop you or block you did not prosper. Remember that healing is a journey, and taking one step at a time is alright. Your invisible scars, the trauma, and the pain that you endured do not define who you are. They are a part of your story of resilience and strength, a testament that you have survived and overcome a challenging experience.

Jesus says He will mend our broken hearts and bind up our wounds. So allow Him to do whatever you need Him to do in your life. Allow Him to heal the invisible scars of your heart. He is doing it for me, and I know He will do the same for you.

4

THERE IS GROWTH THROUGH YOUR PAIN

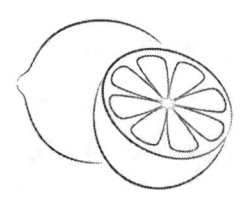

For everything there is a season, and a time for every matter under heaven: a time to be born, and a time to die; a time to plant, and a time to pluck up what is planted; a time to kill, and a time to heal; a time to break down, and a time to build up; a time to weep, and a time to laugh; a time to mourn, and a time to dance.

— ECCLESIASTES 3: 1-4

NO ONE IS SPARED from pain. No one is exempt from grief and experiencing loss. There will come a time in our lives when we will be touched by grief directly or indirectly. We don't just share it when we lose a loved one; People can experience distress at the loss of a job, a pet, a marriage, or a close friendship or relationship. Grief is the reflection of a connection that is no longer there. When a loss happens, it can be debilitating if you allow it to. There are so many emotions that you have to work your way through. Think in terms of having an entangled ball of yarn. You cannot find the beginning or the end of it. It will take a lot of time to untangle it. If you are to be successful at separating the ball of yarn, it will be a process that you must take your time with.

Society has so many unrealistic expectations of how long one should grieve and when one should be over it. There are so many angles to grief that it looks different for everyone. No two people have the same fingerprints, nor do two snowflakes look alike. So, it is the same way with grief. To truly understand something, you must understand what it is not.

Grief is not a task. It is a process. It has no timeline. When it comes to grief, there is no right or wrong way to grieve. For you to grow from your grief, you must allow yourself to go through the pain at your own pace and learn to continue living in a world without that which you have lost.

The world you now live in looks different because things have changed, which you were unprepared for. Finding a healthy and productive way to bring meaning and purpose back into your life would be best.

You cannot take up permanent residence where you currently are. You went someplace in your grief you did not want to go, and you certainly do not want to live there.

I wish we all could have a fairytale ending where we clicked our heels three times, closed our eyes, recited a chant, waved a magic wand, and poof, all our troubles would be over. In reality, it does not happen like that.

You and I can't run or hide from the pain. We must face it for us to grow from it. We aim to run from the pain of the loss; no one likes to feel pain, so we try to steer clear of it by any means necessary. We hope against all hope that things will recalibrate themselves and set everything back in order. We have no other choice but to somehow reclaim our lives. Someone depends on me to pull through this ordeal, and when I do, I will reach out and offer them a firm hand. I will not give up. I can not give up.

This pain of the loss gets unbearable at times. I can hardly stand the weight of it. So I must encourage myself, pull myself up by my bootstrap, square up my shoulders, hold my head up, take a good stance, inhale and exhale, and allow myself to grow through and feel this pain.

I know this is a process, a journey, that I must travel and navigate through challenging terrain. I cannot rush myself or allow others to run me. I cannot heal with I can not feel. The only way through the grief is to go through it. There is no way around it. Jesus tells us that in this world, you will have trouble. But take heart! I have overcome the world. John 6:33 (NIV): Because He has overcome the world, so can we through Him. Understandably, we all will have some trouble in this life. No one is exempt. Without problems, we will not become all we were created to be. We don't grow in the good times. We grow in the tough times, the dark times. Trouble prepares us for the next level. It develops something within us that we cannot get when it's easy, and everything is going well and our way. When the rubber meets the road, our spiritual muscles develop during the hard times. With pain comes growth There is a purpose through your pain. You may need help understanding everything that is going on. According to Romans 8:28, we know that all things work together for good to those who love God and are called according to His purpose. So, trust God's plan even if you don't understand what's happening.

You will bounce back and recover. Restoration is coming your way. Just hold on a bit longer!

5

KNOCKED DOWN BUT NOT KNOCKED OUT!

LIFE IS like a box of chocolates; you never know what you will get. Unlike chocolate, life's tests, trials, tribulations, and challenges are anything but sweet. Dark times will come about in our lifetime and leave a bitter and sour aftertaste. We are unprepared for times that we have not seen from afar. Times when everything around us appears to be falling out of place, and we are in a never-ending free fall without anything to grab hold of.

The bell clanged, signaling the start of a fight I wasn't prepared for. My opponent unleashed a barrage of blows, leaving me reeling. Each jab of misfortune knocked the wind out of me, each cross-punch of hardship pinned me against the ropes of despair.

It was like being caught in a legendary brawl. First, a Muhammad Ali-like setback knocked me out cold. Just as I started to see straight, a Mike Tyson-esque blow landed, taking a precious piece of me with it. Another champion, a Floyd Mayweather of unforeseen challenges, joined the fray. Uppercuts of doubt and hooks of hopelessness rained down, leaving me blinded and gasping for air.

"Lord," I rasped, the white flag of surrender fluttering in my mind. There wasn't an ounce of fight left in me. The cheers of those who believed in me felt muffled, their prayers a distant echo. In the heavy cloud of defeat, I sank, devoid of hope and indifferent to the outcome.

Then, a gentle voice, a lifeline of reason, pierced the darkness. "Patricia," it whispered, reminding me of the fight I still had within. Shame washed over me. I had given up.

With a surge of defiance, I forced my eyes open. The battle may have taken its toll, but I wouldn't surrender without a fight. Taking a deep breath, I reattached the tattered pieces of my spirit and refocused on the challenge. The roar of the crowd, the silent prayers, all came flooding back, urging me to rise. With shaky legs, I stepped back into the ring, ready to fight another round.

I was built for this. I. was made in the battle. You will have to fight some battles. You will have to get in the trenches and dig your way out. You will have scars, bumps, and bruises, but you must never give up on life. Let your scars remind you that you went through something and survived it. Your scar is the proof. Decide not to give up on life. Life will throw you curveballs while standing in the batter's box. Whether you swing the bat or walk back to the dugout is your choice.

Stay in the game of life. YOU MAY GET KNOCKED DOWN, BUT YOU WILL NOT GET KNOCKED OUT. GET UP! GET UP! GET UP!

6

ZIKLAG

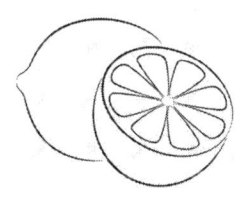

And it came to pass, when David and his men were come to Ziklag on the third day, that the Amalekites had invaded the south, and Ziklag, and smitten Ziklag, and burned it with fire; and had taken the women captives, that were therein: they slew not any, either great or small, but carried them away, and went on their way. So David and his men came to the city, and, behold, it was burned with fire; and their wives, and their their sons, and their daughters, were taken captive. Then David and the people that were with him lifted up their voice and wept, until they had no more power to weep.

— 1 SAMUEL 30:1-4 KJV

CAN YOU IMAGINE THE DISTRESS, discouragement, and despair that David and his men must have felt when all their material possessions were gone and destroyed by fire; all that was left was a smoldering pile of ash. A reminder of what once was? As you stand and look around you, tears streaming down your face, all there is to see is utter destruction and ash. You wonder to yourself, how can I get through this? Everything that I have worked hard for has been lost and destroyed by fire.

All of your hopes, aspirations, and expectations are gone. You stoop down and scoop up the ash of what now remains, and the ash sifts through your fingers as the wind gently blows it away. There will be times when we feel distressed. Situations we can't control will occur, and we will have a Ziklag experience when the seams of life begin to come apart. How do you pick up the pieces and rebuild from the ashes? As you walk around taking inventory of the damage and destruction that has taken place in your life, look at the ruins of what is left. You want things to be like they were before tragedy struck. You are desperately desiring to bring normalcy back into your life.

No one knows the mental and physical anguish, the silent screams, despair, heartaches, all the struggles that you are dealing with in your Ziklag surrounded by broken walls, broken and fragmented pieces, the ash that you must somehow find your way out of so that you can rise and rebuild. Ziklag is the reflection of the loss that has occurred in your life, and the ash is a constant reminder that everything is gone and nothing remains. You may not have the strength to make it out alive or know which way to go. You cannot make it out of Ziklag in your power. The struggle and the weight of it is too much for you to bear on your own. Your Ziklag is a temporary experience; you should not take up permanent residence there. Like David, he encouraged himself in the Lord, and you must do the same. Your strength comes from God. Find your strength in God. God's strength begins when yours is at an end. I will gladly boast about my weaknesses so Christ's power may rest on me. That is why, for Christ's sake, I delight in weaknesses, insults, hardships, persecutions, and difficulties. For when I am weak, then I am strong. 2 Corinthians 12: 9-10.

You can depend on God to see you through. Have strong faith in God; trust Him; his strength is enough. I promise He will bring you through Ziklag and walk with you through the ash and ruins. He is always right by our side to comfort us.

How do I know? I am glad you asked. I know because He is doing it and has done it for me. I have found Him to be faithful to His word.

7

OUT OF SYNC

SYNCHRONIZATION IS the operation of two or more things at the same time. December 20, 2017, is the date the synchronization was interrupted, and things became out of sync. There was a disconnect between my heart and mind. In my mind, I knew that my son's physical presence on this earth had ceased to exist, but in my heart, he was still with me. Things are out of sync; my heart and mind do not agree they are no longer in harmony. Somehow, I put a smile on my face and pretended things were all aligned. Some people may say and think that ample time has passed, and I should be farther along and should let the memory of my son leave. My heart will not allow me to do so even though my mind says otherwise. They are out of sync.

The path that we are on is not a path that we would have chosen for ourselves. This path is a process, not a task, and as we try to get our footing, we will do our best to navigate it. How can I even begin to get my heart and mind synchronized again? I must figure out how to reconnect, assemble what I have left, and bring it back into alignment. My spiritual compass is not functioning correctly; it is spinning out of control. The trajectory of my life has gone in a direction I am unfamiliar with. It has taken a detour that needed to be added to my road map. My mind tells me to give up, but my heart tells me to persevere. My mind tells me all is lost, but my spirit tells me I shall recover. My mind tells me to stop living, but my spirit tells me that I shall live and not die. My mind tells me this is bad, but my heart tells me everything works for my good.

Have you ever sat down in quietness and tried with all your might to hear your child's voice? Have you ever sat at the dinner table and looked at the door, hoping your child would walk through it? Have you had to close your eyes and try to remember the warmth from the hugs of hugging your child and them hugging you back? Have you ever had to look at photos and videos to remember their face and the sound of their voice when they were so full of life? Our minds and intellect know they are no longer with us, but we carry them daily in our hearts. Our hearts and minds are out of sync, and our coordination and balance are not aligned. When the tsunami waves of grief come crashing in and sneak up on us when we go to sleep and wake up the next day, our hearts and minds are out of sync. Our hearts are the bed where our loved ones are safe and secure, and our mind is the thunderbolt that knocks everything out of sync and brings us to the realization that they are no longer here.

If you haven't had to do any of these things or can not relate to what I have said, I envy you because you have something I long for. Only a few people will understand what I am talking about. My life has been knocked off balance and is out of sync. I am walking on a pathway I was unprepared to walk, but since I am here, I will walk it with the Father. The loss of my son does not mean anything to some, but to his family and friends, he meant everything to us. Yes, I still cry after all this time! Yes, I am still grieving and mourning! Yes, I am still very much heartbroken, but most of all, I am a mother with emotions and feelings; a piece of me is forever missing. So before you try to judge and tell me how to feel, how long to grieve, and you think that I should be over it by now. Once you have become qualified and have to bury your child, then maybe you and I can come together and talk. But until that happens, keep your comments, thoughts, opinions, and ideas to yourself.

My mind and heart have been out of sync for quite some time now. I know that God will perfect all that concerns me. The Lord desires that we be made whole. He is our Strength, our Physician, and only Helper that heals our body, soul, spirit, and mind. I give Him all the glory. The Lord has brought me a mighty long way and is keeping me. He has brought me through the snares designed to take me out. His angels are encamped around me. I have found Him to be faithful in all that He does. I could have lost my mind; He is a heart fixer and a mind regulator.

I know that the Lord will bring peace where there is confusion. It is He who will align things according to His perfect will.

In everything, give thanks, for this is the will of God in Christ Jesus concerning you.

—1 THESSALONIANS 5:18

8

I DONT LOOK LIKE WHAT I HAVE BEEN THROUGH

This chapter is taken from Daniel 3: 1-30.

The story of the 3 Hebrew boys: Shadrach, Meshach, and Abednego.

The three Hebrew boys, Shadrach, Meshach, and Abednego, were put in a fiery furnace not because they had done something wrong but because they had done something right. They refused to bow to King Nebuchadnezzar's idol god to worship it; Nebuchadnezzar, full of anger and fury, commanded that the three Hebrew boys be thrown in the fiery furnace, and the furnace should be heated seven times hotter than usual.

Although it is not likely that someone will put us into a physical, fiery furnace, the trials and troubles of life can arrive without warning. They can be overwhelmingly hot, uncomfortable, and discouraging. Whatever stage of life you are in, I am sure you have realized that life is not a bed of roses, nor is it walking in a field of tulips and daisies. Trials of life come in all shapes and sizes; they come unexpectedly and catch you off guard, so don't be surprised when you find yourself in one. We are not free from life's storms, tribulations, tests, and fiery trials.

> *Jesus tells us, these things I have spoken unto you, that in this world you shall have difficulty; but be of good cheer; I have overcome the world.*
>
> — JOHN 6:33

> *Also, a man born of a woman is of few days and full of trouble.*
>
> — JOB 14:1

Trouble will touch all of us, and we will find ourselves in fires burning as we journey through life. When those fires come, we will be tempted to give up, to quit. It's in those fires that we will ask the question why me? What did I do to deserve this? Can anything good come from this? Remember this truth: when you face the fire, you will not face it alone. God is in the fire with you and independently controls the thermostat.

When the guards opened the furnace doors, the fire consumed them; Shadrach, Meshach, and Abednego were not. They were in the fire's midst and didn't smell like smoke. There was no physical evidence that they were even in the fire. They did not look like what they had been through. People see you now, but they didn't see you then. They didn't see the bruises after you had been beaten, the blackeye, the busted eardrums, the broken arm. They didn't see you when you had your teeth knocked out or had a gun put to your head. They didn't see you when you were being raped or molested as a child. They didn't see you when you were hungry with no food to eat, living on the street with no place to call your own; they didn't see you when you were a drug user or an alcoholic. They didn't see the physical, emotional, and mental abuse that you suffered.

They didn't see you when you were in your struggles.

I thank God that I don't look like what I have been through. I thank God you don't look like what you have been through. There are no traces, residue, or evidence to show that you were even in the fire. You can now smile, laugh, live, love again. Your past did not dictate your future. You can rise above your past troubles and circumstances.

If you have been through heartache, hardships, and betrayal, regardless of what you have gone through, there is hope for tomorrow. I thank God for His transformational power, which allowed us to rise above our past struggles. I know that God is in control during a crisis. He brought me through the fiery trials and will do the same for you. You and I will look different from what we have been through. You have been in the fire, but the fire did not consume you. You were in the flood, but the waters did not drown you.

PRAISE GOD YOU SURVIVED. YOU DO NOT LOOK LIKE WHAT YOU BEEN THROUGH! I DONT LOOK LIKE WHAT I HAVE BEEN THROUGH!

Can I trust you with my tears, or will you turn and walk away? Do they offend you, and that's why you can't stay? Do my tears remind you of how short life can be, and it might be you crying instead of me? Can I trust you with my tears, or will you use them against me, pointing them out for all to see? Can I trust you with my tears when they begin to flow, or will you tell me that I should've stopped crying a long time ago? Can I trust you with my tears as they roll down my cheeks when I am without words to speak? Can I trust you with my tears, and you understand my pain, or will you look at me with pity and shame? Can I trust you with my tears, do they bring up your most dreaded fears? Can I trust you to wipe them away, to stand by my side, or will you leave me all alone. My tears are expressions of what I feel, emotions that I can no longer hide. They represent the heartache I feel, which I must embrace as I heal.
CAN I TRUST YOU WITH MY TEARS?

9

HELP IS ON THE WAY

PERHAPS YOU ARE in a season of difficulty and have not gotten the relief you are praying and hoping will manifest. I encourage you to keep pushing, even when it seems useless, even when life doesn't make sense, even when you have cried until you feel like you have no more strength, even when it looks like you have come to the end of the road and there is nowhere to go. When the enemy is telling you that believing God is [pointless and useless, do not believe him because he is a liar; he has been since the beginning of time, and he always will be.I know that sometimes we feel abandoned by God when we go through hard things. Satan tells us that we are not blessed and favored by God. That God is not good and merciful. After all, how could He be when He allows such bad things to happen? I have realized that what seems to be the worst is the best thing for advancing God's kingdom. Everything we go through serves as a divine purpose for our lives. As ugly, unfair, and distasteful as it is, God will use it to glorify Himself and prove that nothing is too hard for Him.

Had not the circumstances shown up in your life, God could not have shown HIs divinity, His deity, His power, and His ability to do the impossible in your life. Whether the problem is big or small, simple or complicated, OUR FATHER CAN SOLVE IT. Our God is enormous, and He is bigger than any issues we are facing. Let me encourage you and tell you that the best is coming. God had to let the problem continue so that He could manifest His divine power. All you have to do is wait on Him and trust Him. He will move by His power and make a way out of no way. God will turn your negative story into a positive testimony. Help is on the way. Just continue to wait on the Lord. Your waiting will pay off. When God moves, you will look back and see He was there all along. He had a plan already in place. You just had to be patient and hang on until the right time for the manifestation of His divine purpose for your life.

God will restore what is broken in your life and give you the strength to pick up the pieces and make something unforgettable from what was shattered. Just wait on Him. Whatever you are facing in your world now, don't focus on what looks like a problem, but focus on the problem solver Jesus. Be mindful that God will perfect what concerns you and work everything out according to His will for your life. God will do the impossible in your life. He will do things that are impossible for man to do. He works behind the scenes. You can't see it now, but you will. He is changing the outcome, shifting circumstances, healing the brokenhearted, restoring what is broken, erasing guilt and shame, and increasing where there is a lack. And it's all for His manifested glory. Help is on the way; continue to wait for the manifestation of God's glory. It is about to happen. When your breakthrough comes, when your supernatural release happens, give God the Praise. All that you have gone through is the push that you need to catapult you to the purpose that God has for you.

Let us pray:

God, the struggles have been difficult, but I will endure them faithfully so you will get the glory through my life. I stand on your word, and the best is yet to come; better days are ahead. I ask you to forgive me of my sins and to come into my life as my Lord and Saviour. And when my breakthrough is revealed I will carefully give your name the honor, praise, and glory. It all belongs to you.

In Jesus name, Amen.

When I found out you were in my womb, I was overjoyed with anticipation of meeting you soon; knowing for the moment you were safe and secure, I never gave a moment thought of the pain I would endure, I can't wait to hold you, kiss you, and look into the face of the little one that's occupying this space, I often imagine of how life would be for the little person that's growing inside of me, I promise to be there for the good and bad, from the beginning to the end, I am not just your mother I am your friend, I had our lives all planned of how it would be, but God had other plans that I did not see, I remember the talks we had in response you would kick your feet, waiting patiently until last we meet, suddenly something happened I do not know that cease life inside to grow, I will forever love you with all my heart, it will always carry you and we shall never be apart.
LOVE LIVE ON IT NEVER DIES!

10

RIZPAH

It is in 2 Samuel 21:1 that we are introduced to Rizpah. Rizpah is a mother who is grieving and mourning over the premature and untimely death of her two sons. Rizpah's sons were brutally and violently slaughtered along with five other family members in a vengeful act of retaliation against their father, King Saul.

Rizpah two sons whom she bore unto Saul, and the five grandsons of Saul were all taken, and the Gibeonites hung them in the hills before the Lord, and all seven together were put to death in the days of the harvest, in the first days, at the beginning of barley harvest. And Rizpah took sackcloth and spread it upon the rock, from the beginning of harvest until water dropped (rain) from heaven and did not allow the birds of the air to rest on them by day, nor the animals of the field by night. 2

Samuel 21:3-10. Rizpah had a front-row seat to seeing her two sons violently murdered before her very eyes. All she could do at that very moment was stand and watch; she was voiceless and powerless; there wasn't anything she could do to stop King David from taking her sons and using them as a sacrifice to please the Gibeonites.

So she proceeds to do the only thing that she can do as she watches her son's defiled, decaying, and swollen bodies hanging exposed to the elements. She protects her son's body after death by sitting vigil for five months, keeping the birds (vultures) away during the daytime and the beasts of the field by night (lions, tigers, and bears) away from them.

Although she could not protect them while they were living, in their death, she is a faithful mother in protecting their bodies. As parents, mothers, fathers, and grandparents, we would do all that is humanly possible to protect our children and grandchildren and prevent any harm from happening to them.

I, too, was like Rizpah; I was powerless to stop my son from being murdered. If I were there, without any hesitation, I would have jumped in front of the gun and taken the bullet that was aimed at my son. As parents, this is just an instinct because we are always the protectors of our children, no matter their age. Rizpah vigil after her son's death is silent; her grief and mourning give witness to her son's death. The king took notice of it, removed their bodies, and gave them a proper burial. As parents who have lost children, we are much like Rizpah; we want our grief to be witnessed. We want people to know that our children mattered, were and still are loved, and did exist. Most importantly, we want people to know that we are not broken, that we don't need fixing, that we are parents who are grieving our children, and that this is what grief looks like.

I cannot even begin to imagine what Rizpah must have felt watching the execution of her sons. They were killed because of a vengeful retaliation for someone else's wrongdoing. They were found guilty by association. Saul was their father, and they lost their lives because of a broken promise.

In today's society of social media, there have been so many parents and families that have unfortunately witnessed the death of their child or children and were powerless to stop it. They are modern-day Rizpahs. When they watch the video footage from the convenience store, the Facebook live recording, and the evening news, they have front-row seating and are powerless because there isn't anything they could have done to stop it. So, like Rizpah, we will not give up. We will continue vigil by seeking justice until someone notices; we will continue to be our children's voices. Like

Rizpah, we will come together and form support groups, become public speakers and advocates, get involved, and try to pass laws and legislation seeking justice for all those who are unjustly executed until someone listens and takes notice.

We are Rizpah; although we can no longer protect our children who are no longer with us, we can preserve and honor their memories by trying to save others, keep vigil, and keep them from harm.

Rizpah's love for her sons did not die with them because love lives on, and neither does ours.

11

MARY'S LEMONS: A MOTHER'S AGONY AT THE CRUCIFIXION OF JESUS

JESUS CHRIST'S crucifixion is a pivotal (turning point) event in Christian history, symbolizing sacrifice, redemption, and the ultimate triumph of love over suffering. Among the witnesses to this intense moment was Mary, the mother of Jesus. As a devoted mother, Mary's emotions during her son's crucifixion were undoubtedly complex and overwhelming.

Mary's love for her son was profound, and witnessing his death would have caused great sorrow and grief. As a mother, she nurtured and cared for Jesus from infancy, witnessing his growth and development. Seeing him suffer and die in such a brutal manner would have shattered her heart, causing her unimaginable pain. Her presence at the crucifixion shows her powerlessness to intervene and save her son. Despite her deep love and desire to protect him, she was unable to prevent his arrest, trial, and crucifixion. This sense of helplessness would have added to her anguish as she was forced to watch her beloved child endure unimaginable suffering.

Mary's faith in God and understanding of Jesus' divine mission may have provided solace during this difficult time. As a devout follower of God, she may have found solace in believing that Jesus' sacrifice was part of a GREATER PLAN FOR HUMANITY'S SALVATION. Her unwavering faith would have given her the strength to endure the pain and anguish of witnessing her son's death. Her presence at the foot of the cross demonstrates her steadfast support for him, even in his darkest hour. She remained by his side despite her suffering, offering him comfort and love. Her compassion and empathy for Jesus, the other crucified criminals, and the crowd exemplify her selflessness and deep maternal love.

While Mary's grief and sorrow were no doubt overwhelming, her faith in God's plan may have instilled a sense of hope and resilience within her. She may have found comfort in the belief that Jesus' sacrifice would ultimately lead to the redemption of humanity. This hope would have given her the strength to continue spreading

Jesus' message of love and forgiveness. However, Mary experienced a wide range of emotions during her son's crucifixion. Her spiritual strength, compassion, and unwavering faith balanced her sorrow, helplessness, and grief. Despite the immense pain she endured, Mary's presence at the foot of the cross symbolizes her unconditional love and support for her son, as well as her commitment to GOD'S PLAN FOR HUMANITY'S SALVATION. During this tragic event, her story serves as a testament to the enduring power of a mother's love, portraying her as a figure of unwavering love, faith, and strength in the face of great suffering.

Mary's Lemonade: John 10:18 Jesus says,

> *No one takes my life from me. I give it up willingly. I can give it up and receive it back again, just as my father commanded me to.*

Jesus offered himself on the cross to pay the price for humanity's sins, reconciling humanity with God. Through his crucifixion and resurrection, Jesus has provided a way for humanity to be redeemed and saved from sin and its consequences. His sacrifice is a means of offering salvation and eternal life to those who believe in him. Jesus' sacrifice is the ultimate demonstration of God's love for humanity. By willingly undergoing immense suffering and death on the cross, Jesus exemplified selfless love and sacrifice, serving as a model for us to follow in our own lives. Both the crucifixion and resurrection of Jesus are a triumph over death and evil. Those who believe in His name believe that we have the promise of eternal life through His death and resurrection.

HANNAH

IN ANCIENT BIBLE DAYS, having children was considered a blessing from the Lord. If a woman could not conceive or give birth, she was disgraced, shunned, and looked down on by other women because it meant that she was not able to fulfill her God-given purpose of producing offspring for her husband.

HANNAH'S LEMONS: Hannah was such a woman; she was barren and unable to conceive a child for a long time for her husband, Elkanah. Her infertility had caused her humiliation and shame. This disgrace and humiliation had left a bitter, sour, and distasteful taste in Hannah's mouth. For years, Hannah poured out her heart's desire to the Lord in prayer. She yearned for a son but couldn't conceive. Year after year, Hannah would go to the temple and petition the Lord for a son, and year after year,

Penninah would shame her because of her infertility situation. Hannah promised the Lord that if he would give her a son, she promised that she would give the child back to the Lord.

Not only did Hannah have to deal with the humiliation of being ridiculed because of her barrenness, but for years, she was bullied and grievously irritated by Peninnah, her husband Elkanah's other wife. Because the Lord had closed Hannah's womb, she couldn't bear children. But Peninnah had many children for Elkanah, and she made sure that she reminded Hannah of this fact.

The life that Hannah endured was one of sorrow and bitterness. Still, despite her strength, courage, persistent prayer, and unwavering commitment to seeking God's face, she did not stop praying despite the lemons that life had given her. In her season of opposition, strife, continuous shaming, disgrace, and ridicule, Hannah took the lemons given to her (barrenness). She squeezed them with resiliency in seeking God, persistence in prayer, having faith in God, and speaking victory despite her current situation.

HANNAH'S LEMONADE: After she had suffered for a while, God mended what was broken; he restored, established, and strengthened Hannah, and she gave birth to a son and named him Samuel, which means God has heard.

When Samuel was weaned, Hannah kept her promise to give the child to God in service to Him. She took Samuel to the temple to live with Eli, the priest, and Eli promised to take good care of him. Samuel grew up in the sight of the Lord.

The Lord God was gracious to Hannah; this is the sweetest lemonade; she gave birth to three sons and two daughters.

13

FROM LEMONS TO LIFE: A DEVOTIONAL ON FAITH AND RESTORATION

IMAGINE A LIFE SQUEEZED DRY, leaving nothing but the bitter tang of lemons. This wasn't just a metaphor for the widow of Zarephath; it was the harsh reality she lived with every empty breath. Poverty had stolen away any semblance of comfort. Each day was a struggle to find enough scraps to keep her thin frame fueled. But the true drought, the one that parched her soul, was the loss of her son.

He had been her sunrise, chasing away the shadows of loneliness with his laughter. Now, her home echoed with a deafening silence, a constant reminder of the future stolen away. Grief clung to her like a suffocating blanket of darkness.

Life had given her lemons. The bitterness of loss was in everything she touched and in every corner of her home. Each room, held a memory that would slowly, over the years, fade away into nothingness.

Yet, even in her despair, a single, a seed of faith remained. Perhaps it was a memory whispered in the quiet moments before dawn, a promise of a kind and loving God heard long ago. This tiny seed, fragile as it seemed, held the potential to blossom into something extraordinary.

When Elijah, the prophet of God, appeared on her doorstep, the widow saw more than just another hungry mouth to feed. In that moment, a spark ignited within her. Here, in the face of her own desperate situation, was an opportunity.

Filled with grief and anger, the widow confronts Elijah, questioning why God would bring more suffering after she had shown such faith. This reaction is understandable. Sometimes, when faced with new setbacks, it's easy to forget the promises we hold onto. We might even feel like God has abandoned us.

But here's the beauty of the story: Elijah doesn't condemn the widow's doubt. Instead, he takes action. He prays fervently, and through his prayer, the boy is miraculously brought back to life. This act serves as a powerful symbol. It shows us that God doesn't always prevent hardship, but He is always present, working in ways we may not understand. Sometimes, the "lemonade" He offers comes in the form of unexpected blessings, a reminder of His love and power to restore even the most broken things.

So, the next time life throws you lemons, remember the widow of Zarephath. Remember that even in the darkest moments, faith can be a catalyst for hope. And trust that God, in His perfect timing, will bring sweetness to your situation, even if it doesn't look the way you expect.

The widow's story reminds us that:

Hope isn't a fleeting feeling; it's a promise etched in stone by God. He promises to provide and restore, and His faithfulness endures like a lighthouse in a storm. The widow's son may not have been the answer to her every prayer, but God's love and power were undeniably present. Just as He breathed life back into the boy, He can breathe new life into our situations. He can use our challenges to strengthen our faith and draw us closer to Him.

Through God, we can go from Lemons to Legacy.

So, the next time life hands you lemons, remember the widow of Zarephath. Take a stand in faith, trust in God's promises, and watch Him work in unexpected ways. You may lose a loved one, and their physical presence may not return. But that doesn't mean God won't bring life from that loss. He has infinite ways to help you make lemonade with those lemons. Perhaps He'll bring new connections, unexpected blessings, or a deeper understanding of His love. Trust that even in the face of hardship, He is working a purpose in your life, a legacy born from your pain.

14

LEMONADE

THERE IS a proverbial phrase that says when life gives you lemons, make lemonade. Lemons represent the negative things in life, the sourness or difficulties we experience. Making lemonade out of lemons means that whatever problems, adversities, or challenges we have, we should use them to make something good. Lemons are bitter and sour, leaving a nasty after-taste in our mouth, which isn't pleasant.

The following stories are just a few out of many that have made lemonade out of lemons. These stories will reflect the resilience, courage, and strength the individuals possessed to overcome the adversity they experienced. When life offered them lemons, they decided to make lemonade and share it with others. They took a negative experience and turned it into something positive.

* * *

Raven Lemon story: In 1996, at the tender age of 12 1/2, she witnessed her mother being fatally shot to death due to domestic gun violence as she hid in the bushes along with her younger siblings, ages 9 and 5, trying to protect them.

Raven's Lemonade: Today, Raven is 40 years old. She is thriving and works in the medical field. She owns rental property and her home, which is 1 1/2 acres. Raven is a SURVIVOR

* * *

Jae Honey Lemon story: Jae's daughter Carieal was murdered on April 14, 2020, at the age of 18; her daughter's friend murdered her daughter. The young man would come over, hang out with Jae's daughter, and eat dinner with the family. He shot Carieal in the back of the head. She never had a chance; she never saw it coming.

Jae's Lemonade: Today, Jae Honey is the author of Six Minutes of Freedom Surviving The Loss Of A Child. She hosts the annual prom at the high school her daughter graduated from in honor of Carieal. Also, she hosts a yearly fun day at the city park in honor of Cariel.

Jae also facilitates Poetry through the Pain Support Group. She's also active in the Losing Isaiah Support Group, where she aids another mother with this group. Jae facilitates a support group for siblings to help them navigate losing a sibling. Lastly, Jae is a member of Woodson's Center Voices of Black Mother United Support (VBMU) group, which assists individuals and organizations in family advocacy, community intervention, and promoting positive policing (PPP). Jae is persevering through adversity; She is a SURVIVOR.

* * *

NANCY BOKMA LEMONS: Nancy's son Justin was murdered on July 01, 2016, in a nightclub. Currently, there has been no arrest in the death of her son; no one has come forward with any information that will lead to a conviction.

Nancy Lemonade: She is transforming. She had to believe she would become a better person on the other side. She owned her grief, and, like the phoenix, she rose from the ashes. She has engaged herself in self-care, going back and learning from the past to enable herself to move forward. Nancy is Justin's voice and continues to seek justice and keep his legacy alive. Nancy continues to write her next chapter. She is a SURVIVOR.

* * *

DeEDRA LEMONS: DeEdra's son Ryan and his best friend Greg were murdered on July 26, 2017.

DeEdra Lemonade: De Edra has started a support group for siblings to help them talk about their loss. So often, the sibling gets overlooked, and all the focus is directed to the parents. DeEdra noticed that this happened with Ryan's siblings, and she has become proactive in helping siblings by offering them a place to talk and get support through their grief. She is a SURVIVOR.

* * *

ZANETIA LEMONS: ZANETIA'S SON DRE' was murdered on April 26, 2019.

Zanetia Lemonade: Since the tragic loss of her son Dre, Zanetia has been very proactive. She is the CEO of Operation Recovery Inc., whose mission is to support grieving parents emotionally, mentally, physically, and financially. She is also the lead representative for Mississippi for the Woodson's Center Voices of Black Mother's United (VBMU), whose mission is to assist individuals and organizations in family advocacy, community intervention, and promoting positive policing (PPP).

She is also active in Mother Against Gang Violence, whose mission is to connect families with community resources and assist at-risk youth with making better decisions, improving their behavior, and avoiding gang involvement. Zanetia is also a motivational speaker who can enter the school system and talk with school-age children about being positive role models within the community, pursuing an education, and avoiding gang affiliations. She is a SURVIVOR.

* * *

Rhonda Lemons: Rhonda is a survivor of rape and attempted murder, and she was stabbed in the eye by her attacker, among other horrific things.

Rhonda's Lemonade: Today, Rhonda is a published author of The Blessed Survivor, a must-read book that tells of surviving a horrendous attack on her life. She is also the CEO of Lady Knight Enterprises Publishing. She is a motivational speaker and minister. She has been heard on several radio shows like the Russ Parr morning show (nationally syndicated) and several TV shows, including Atlanta Live. She's been a radio and Television personality and producer of the UPLIFTING television show and International Radio Show, giving survivors a voice while impacting the world for positive change. She is a SURVIVOR.

***

Corinna Lemons: Corinna's son was murdered on May 27, 2020.

Corinna Lemonade: It was hard, but I served my way through. I could embrace every moment with the understanding that God was in control, and I trusted His process. My son's death sparked my desire to push SWAT, "Surviving with a testimony," a ministry where I talk to youth and parents about choices they make and how gun violence changes the entire family dynamic. I was able to turn my pain into my passion by starting my own business, Snazzy's Designs and Events, where I can bring the vision of my customers to life whether it is a wedding, birthday party, baby shower, or bridal shower, or something as simple as a gift basket for any occasion.

***

Brenda's Lemons: Brenda's son, Yasin, was murdered.

Brenda Lemonade: It was a simple prayer request I prayed for continuously night after night. Lord, please get my son. I need you to be with my son; I can not rest until you show me my son. I was in a dark, downward place but never questioned the Lord. But I just continued praying that He would deliver my son, go and get him, and show me that he was in His presence. The night He brought my son to me, it was raining, and a bright light shone on him. Yasin came to me dressed up and working on a pickup truck, and he told me not to worry about his soul because God had him working in the field.

From that day on, I have thanked God for who He is. The Lord is worthy to be praised. Turn your lemons into prayer, and you will receive the sweetest lemonade ever. She is a SURVIVOR

* * *

PATRICIA'S LEMONS: Patricia's son was murdered on December 20, 2017, on his 26th birthday.

Patricia's Lemonade: Today, I am an assistant Pastor and author of 4 books: 926 Sustaining Faith, 37 to Life, The Aftermath That Led to Victory, Caution Reckless When Open, and When Life Gives You Lemons, Make A Legacy. I am the founder of MMAD Support Group. MMAD is a non-profit organization birthed from a place of pain with a call to action. After experiencing the traumatic loss of my son to gun violence in 2017, I felt a strong unction to make a difference. MMAD is the fruition of a promise that I made to my son. I promised him that his death would not be in vain and that I would make a difference. I had a desire to try and help other parents who need support, who need to talk about their loss, and who need help to navigate through the trauma of the death of a child. It is a support group designed to unite and offer support and encouragement to parents with common problems and experiences. MMAD is an emotional support group for grieving parents. In addition to the MMAD support group, I also created a private online group via Facebook, Voices Against Violence (Parents of Murdered Children.) where parents can come and feel safe and comfortable about sharing any feelings they are experiencing. It is a nonjudgemental group. Also, I am pursuing a BS in psychology and crisis counseling because I want to help those who are hurting.

* * *

THE THINGS we have experienced have left a bitter and sour taste in our mouths, but we took the negative (painful) stuff of life and used it to make something (sweet) lemonade.

AFTERWORD

I am the author of 926 Sustaining Faith; 37 to Life: The Aftermath That Led to Victory; Caution Reckless When Open; and When Life Gives You Lemons, Make A Legacy. I wrote these books as they were written and birthed from a place of pain. On December 20, 2017, my only son was murdered on his 26th birthday, and this was the moment the trajectory of my life drastically changed, and I discovered that there is purpose in my pain.

Some things were locked inside of me that I wasn't aware of. Experiencing the death of my son was the push that moved me out of my comfort zone, and I began to walk into my purpose. This journey of recovery gets very uncomfortable and scary at times because I am walking in unfamiliar and uncharted territory while trying to

AFTERWORD

avoid explosive landmines. I have never traveled this way before. God is my compass, and I depend on Him to be a light unto my pathway as I travel this sometimes dark path. He continues to sustain me as He has done from the beginning, He continues to give me strength, and His grace is sufficient for me. God has given me the ability to write these books for His glory, and I thank him for it all.

The objective of these books is to encourage people and to let them know that there is hope and that we are not alone in our struggles, hardships, and difficulties. No matter how hot and intense the journey becomes, you will not be consumed by the fiery trial you go through. You will emerge on the other side of your difficulties. To truly grasp and understand my journey, you must start at the beginning of when it all began. 926 Sustaining Faith; 37 To Life: The Aftermath That Led To Victory; Caution Reckless When Open; and the book you are currently reading. The books are a sequel and must be read in the order in which events occurred. I am very transparent in my writing and show my vulnerability and frailty. Still, most importantly, they portray the mighty hand of God, His ability and strength that continues to carry me through the healing process. Healing does not mean forgetting; healing is a reminder that we went through an ordeal and survived.

AFTERWORD

The tragic events that took place on that date have brought me to the place I am today to my purpose. I have written four books and created an online private group for parents to talk and get support from other parents. I facilitate a grief and bereavement group in my community (MMAD), Mother Making A Difference.

I Give God All The Glory

ABOUT THE AUTHOR

Patricia Morgan lives in Poplarville, Mississippi . She is the mother of three children Quontelis, Patreceia, and David Gilmore, Jr in whose memory this book is written. Patricia is the author is 926 sustaining faith, and 37 to life the aftermath that led to victory.

Patricia is a woman who has stood strong in her faith, and she continues to trust in God to order her steps. She knows that every one of her steps are a process that she must go through and that those steps are all for the Glory of God. She continues to trust God's plan for her life even when she does not understand what is going on.

Patricia has found God to be faithful and that is why she will forever trust him.

Patricia lives with her family in the Poplarville area.

Patricia is the founder **of MMAD Support Group for Grieving Parents.**

Follow her author journey at: https://books2read.com/Patricia-Morgan

MMAD is a non-profit organization that was birthed from a place of pain with a call to action. After experiencing the traumatic loss of my son due to gun violence in 2017. I felt a strong unction to make a difference. MMAD is the fruition of a promise that I made to my son. I promised him that his death would not be in vain. I had to act and make a difference. I felt the unction to try and help other parents. Mothers and fathers that need support, that need to talk about their loss, and need help to navigate through the trauma of the death of a child.

MMAD is an emotional support group for grieving parents that is designed to bring together and facilitate support and encouragement amongst parents who share common problems and experiences.

ABOUT THE PUBLISHER

LAK**E**V**i**EW
PUBLICATIONS

"Everyone has a story to tell, only the courageous will find a way to get it told. Let my team and I help you become courageous!"

Helping people become courageous is something we have been doing since LakeView Publications was founded in 2018.

With every author we have helped since book one, I am reminded of the day I decided to take the big step of writing my first book. I was quickly overwhelmed with trying to figure out how to bring my dream to life, I just knew that I had a message to share with the world. If you are like I was, You are *NOT* alone! Nearly 100% of our clients started with an idea but had no idea what to do with their idea. That is where my team and I come in. We publish AMAZING books written by AMAZING people who had an idea and took a step in courage to ask the right question. The best way to start, or at least get the next steps is to ask the most important question.

How Do I Get My Book Published?

Finding the right publisher is key. The team at LakeView Publications is driven by our passion to help people tell their stories and in helping them find a way to allow their story to take them to the next level. One of the greatest parts about assisting people in the publishing journey of their story is being able to connect with them and help them find their voice. You reach out to us with the best way to reach you, and we do the rest. It's that easy!

You wrote the book; we do everything else!

When you contact us, we will find out where you are in the process and give you an assessment of what you will need to get you from where you are to where you want to be!

Our team is absolutely magnificent, and they are dedicated to excellence. We offer proofing, editing, layout design, ghostwriting, art illustration, storyboard layout, content coaching, graphic design, and everything else you may need to get your book published and released.

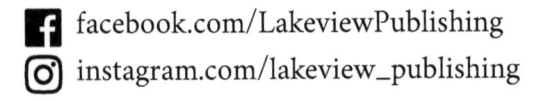

facebook.com/LakeviewPublishing
instagram.com/lakeview_publishing

Want to Publish Your Book?

We Can Help!

* Manuscript Editing

* Book Cover

* Book Formatting

*Illustrations

* Publishing through all major retailers
(Amazon, Kobo, B&N, Apple)

* Paperbacks & eBooks

* Blurb Writing

* Audio Books

* Choose Your Own Package

* Author Retains <u>ALL</u> rights

We're here to help!

"Everyone has a story to tell, only the courageous will find a way to get it told. Let my team and I help you become courageous!"

LAKEVIEW
PUBLICATIONS

www.LakeviewPublishers.com

Made in the USA
Columbia, SC
09 June 2024